I KNOW AMERICA

Our National Parks

Michael Weber

THE MILLBROOK PRESS
Brookfield, Connecticut

Published by The Millbrook Press
2 Old New Milford Road
Brookfield, CT 06804
© 1994 Blackbirch Graphics, Inc.

10 9 8 7 6 5 4 3 2 1

Created and produced in association with Blackbirch Graphics.
Series Editor: Tanya Lee Stone

Library of Congress Cataloging-in-Publication Data
Weber, Michael (Michael L.)
    Our national parks / by Michael Weber.
    p.   cm.   — (I know America)
    Includes bibliographical references and index.
    Summary: Describes our country's national parks, the establishment of the National Park Service, and the problems facing our parks today.
    ISBN 1-56294-438-X (lib. bdg.)
    1. National parks and reserves—United States—Juvenile literature. I. Title. II. Series.
E160.W43   1994
973—dc20
                                                      93-35014
                                                           CIP
                                                            AC

Acknowledgments and Photo Credits
Cover, pp. 6, 8, 10, 11, 12, 17, 19, 30: Richard Frear/National Park Service; p. 4: ©Bruce Glassman; pp. 5, 24, 32: National Park Service; pp. 21, 22: Department of Travel Development, Frankfort, KY; pp. 26, 39: John M. Kauffmann/National Park Service; pp. 29, 41: Keller/National Park Service; pp. 33, 36: M. Woodbridge Williams/National Park Service; pp. 34, 44: Cecil W. Stoughton/U.S. Department of Interior; p. 42: Fred Mang, Jr./National Park Service; p. 43: Cecil W. Stoughton/National Park Service.

CONTENTS

The Statue of Liberty is a national treasure and is preserved by the National Park Service.

The United States is a land of great natural beauty, where rivers and lakes abound, tall mountains rise high above the ground, and a wide variety of plants and animals live. To guarantee that all of these resources would not be spoiled in any way by humans, and thus be preserved for future generations, the government began establishing national parks in 1872. Yellowstone National Park, in Wyoming, Montana, and Idaho, was the first national park. Since its establishment in 1872, fifty other areas have been declared national parks.

National parks can be found in all regions of the United States and in the territories of American Samoa and the Virgin Islands. Some are located in the mountains, some in the plains, and others along the Atlantic and Pacific coasts. The climate within the parks varies widely, from the warm, semitropical weather of Florida's Everglades, to the extreme cold of

Alaska's Denali National Park. Many of the parks seem far from civilization, but a few, like Hot Springs in Arkansas, are right in a city.

America's fifty-one national parks are managed by the National Park Service, which is also responsible for many other places in the National Park System— national monuments, forest preserves, historic sites, battlefields, memorials, seashores and lakeshores, and recreation areas. The Statue of Liberty in New York Harbor and the Civil War battlefield at Gettysburg, Pennsylvania, for example, are managed by the National Park Service. The National Park Service has two main goals—to preserve the natural and cultural riches of the United States and to provide visitors to the parks with both recreational and educational experiences.

In this book, you will read about twelve of these beautiful and fascinating parks in four major groups of states: the eastern states, the states that lie between the Appalachian and Rocky mountains, the Rocky Mountain states, and the Pacific states.

America's national parks, such as Yellowstone, offer many stunning views of our country's wilderness.

5

1

THE EASTERN STATES

There are seven eastern national parks. Six are located within the United States proper. A seventh park is in the Virgin Islands, a U.S. territory that lies between the Caribbean Sea and the Atlantic Ocean. Of these seven parks, the state of Florida boasts three: Biscayne, Everglades, and Dry Tortugas, which was established in 1992 and is the newest park. Extending across the border between North Carolina and Tennessee is Great Smoky Mountains National Park, which receives more visitors than any other national park. The other two eastern parks are Shenandoah in Virginia and Acadia in Maine.

Great variety exists among these parks. The Florida parks are largely semitropical and have a lot of water. Biscayne National Park consists mostly of coral reefs and water and contains thirty-three islands.

Opposite:
This photograph captures the breathtaking natural beauty of Everglades National Park at sunset.

Acadia is also nearly surrounded by water, but it is in the much cooler waters of the North Atlantic Ocean. And Great Smoky Mountains National Park and Shenandoah National Park are both mountain parks.

Acadia National Park

Acadia, a place of rocky coasts, crashing waves, lakes, forests, and mountains, is the only national park in the northeastern United States. Located along the coast of Maine, Acadia is almost completely surrounded by water. Most of the park's nearly 42,000 acres are on Mount Desert Island. The remainder is on part of Isle au Haut, several smaller islands, and the Schoodic Peninsula on the mainland. Rising more than 1,500 feet above sea level on Mount Desert Island is Cadillac Mountain, the highest point on the Atlantic coast of the United States.

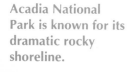

Acadia National Park is known for its dramatic rocky shoreline.

Many places in Acadia National Park show the power of the sea. Thunder Hole is a gash in the rock through which waves crash. At the Seawall, rocks flung by waves have formed a natural dam that separates a saltwater pond from the ocean.

Acadia has many tidal pools with fascinating marine life. At Anemone Cave on Mount Desert Island, you can see starfish, sea anemones, and sea urchins. The park is also home to a variety of wildlife, including bald eagles, beavers, and bobcats.

Many of the activities in Acadia involve water. There is excellent fishing. Boat cruises around the park offer superb views of its scenery. In summer, you can go swimming, but Maine's water is cold! You can also take nature walks and ride horses. Driving along Park Loop Road on the eastern part of Mount Desert Island is a good way to see the park.

Abnaki Indians lived in the area as long as 6,000 years ago. The first white person known to have seen the region was Italian explorer Giovanni da Verrazano in 1500. A Frenchman, Samuel de Champlain, explored the area more thoroughly in 1604.

The name *Acadia* comes from the language of the Micmac Indians. The French used the name in the 1600s for what is now Maine and much of eastern Canada. France ruled the area until 1763, when it became British. Twenty years later, the southern portion became part of the new United States.

In the 1800s, artists began going to the area to draw and paint its beauties. Later in the century,

Acadia became a fashionable place for rich Americans to have summer homes. But people became worried that the region's beauty might be spoiled by over-development. As a result, John D. Rockefeller and other wealthy people donated their lands to the U.S. government. In 1916, Congress made the area a national monument named after Sieur de Monts, a Frenchman who had promoted French colonies in the region in the early 1600s. In 1919, Sieur de Monts National Monument became Lafayette National Park, which became Acadia National Park in 1929.

Everglades National Park

The Everglades provides a home for alligators and crocodiles, many of which were killed for their hides before they were protected by preservation laws.

In the Everglades, the climate is both semitropical (hot and humid) and temperate (mild). The park's 1.5 million acres include forests of cypress, pine, and mangrove, islands, swampy vegetation, and lots of water. The Seminole Indians called the area *Pa-hay-okee*, meaning "grassy water."

Hundreds of birds—pelicans, wood ibis, and egrets—live in the park. Panthers, manatees (air-breathing mammals that live in water and are also called sea cows), snakes, alligators, and crocodiles can be found there, too. Many of these animals exist today only in small numbers and are protected by law.

The Everglades is a paradise for fishermen, but boating, hiking, swimming, and camping are also available. There are five canoe "trails." The longest, Wilderness Waterway, is 100 miles. One of the best walks is along Anhinga Trail. Another highlight is

Cape Sable, the southernmost point on the U.S. mainland, which has both beaches and desert vegetation.

The earliest Everglades Native Americans that we know about were the Calusas and the Tequestas. In the late 1700s, various nations of the Creek Indian Confederation were being crowded out of Georgia and Alabama by the growing white population. Many settled in Florida and came to be known as the Seminoles.

A large portion of the Everglades is covered with swampy vegetation, home to a wide variety of wildlife.

Over the next century, Florida's economic development began to threaten the beauty of the area. Birds were shot so their plumes could be used in women's hats. In addition, cypress, mahogany, and royal palms were cut down for building materials.

In response, a movement was started to preserve the area. Royal Palm State Park was created in 1916. In 1923, the National Park Service recommended the establishment of a national park that was even larger than the state park. In 1934, Congress authorized the national park. But there still was no money to buy the additional land from its owners. In 1946, however, the Florida legislature provided $2 million, and some of the owners donated their lands. Finally, in 1947, Everglades National Park was established.

But even today care must be taken to protect the Everglades. Its beauty and the delicate balance among its plants, animals, land, and water can be easily damaged by human activity.

Great Smoky Mountains National Park

Great Smoky Mountains National Park, established in 1934, is the most popular of all the national parks. During 1992, nearly nine million people visited it.

The park, with more than 520,000 acres, lies in the Great Smoky Mountains, on both sides of the border between Tennessee and North Carolina.

The Great Smokies are part of the Appalachian Mountain chain, which runs from Maine to Alabama. The name *Smoky* comes from the mist that often floats over the mountaintops and hangs in the valleys.

The Great Smokies are the highest mountains in the United States east of the Mississippi River. In the park are sixteen peaks that are more than 6,000 feet high. The Great Smoky Mountains are also among the oldest mountains on earth. They contain rocks that are more than 500 million years old.

Great Smoky Mountains National Park has more than 100 kinds of trees and 3,500 varieties of plant life. In some places, the forest floor is so thickly

Visitors can see the park's plant and animal life by walking the 900 miles of hiking trails in Great Smoky Mountains National Park.

THE MOST POPULAR NATIONAL PARKS

America's fifty-one national parks are great tourist attractions because they are beautiful and interesting. Every year, millions of Americans—and many people from other countries—visit the parks. In 1992, the parks were visited by a total of 57,935,902 people. Listed here are the five parks that received the greatest number of visitors in 1992.

Great Smoky Mountains: 8,931,690
Grand Canyon: 4,203,545
Yosemite: 3,819,518
Yellowstone: 3,144,405
Olympic: 3,030,195

In 1992, visitors to the more than three hundred places managed by the National Park Service numbered 274,694,549.

Source: National Park Service

carpeted with azalea, laurel, and rhododendron plants that these areas are impossible to pass through.

The park is also rich in wildlife. Bears are frequently found in the summer along the highways. Also seen are foxes, deer, and bobcats. There are also many birds, and fish are plentiful in the park's 600 miles of streams.

Cherokee Indians once lived on the lands that now make up Great Smoky Mountains National Park. One Cherokee leader, Attakullakulla, made a trip to see London, England, in the 1730s. Another, Sequoia, invented a writing system for the Cherokee language.

As the number of white settlers grew in the early 1800s, the Cherokees were forced to move. In the park today, Cherokee Indian Village shows how the Cherokees lived. There also are cabins in the Cades Cove area that once were the homes of white settlers.

FROM THE APPALACHIANS TO THE ROCKIES

Within the vast area extending from the Appalachian Mountains in the East to the Rocky Mountains in the West, there are nine national parks. Eight lie in remote areas, hundreds of miles from the nearest city. Only Hot Springs National Park in Arkansas is in the middle of a city. Voyageurs National Park in Minnesota borders Canada, while Big Bend National Park in Texas is directly across from Mexico.

The parks have deep forests, cool lakes, deserts, mountains, caves, and unusual land formations. Isle Royale National Park in Michigan has more water than land. At the other extreme, some parts of Guadalupe Mountains National Park in Texas are so dry that some animals there almost never drink water.

Opposite:
Big Bend National Park was established in 1944 by the National Park Service. It is named for the U-shaped bend of the Rio Grande at Big Bend's site.

15

There is much to see and do in these parks. At Theodore Roosevelt National Park in North Dakota, you can visit the former president's ranch. A boat ride on an underground river awaits you at Mammoth Cave National Park in Kentucky. And in Hot Springs National Park, you can bathe in water that comes out of the ground as warm as bath water.

Badlands National Park

This park is located on nearly 243,000 acres in southwestern South Dakota. In 1939, it was designated a national monument, and in 1978 it became a national park. Most people who have come to the area have been struck by the harsh appearance of the land. Sioux Indians called it *mako sica*, meaning "bad land."

The land has undergone significant changes through the ages. Over millions of years, great disturbances shook the area, causing the land to buckle. As a result, the Rocky Mountains were created a few hundred miles to the west. Later, large amounts of volcanic ash fell on the area. Rain averages only about 15 inches a year. Winters are very cold with blizzards, and summers are very hot. Erosion, the process whereby soil, rocks, and other features of the land are worn away by natural forces like rain and wind, has also contributed to the changing face of the Badlands. As a result of these changes, the park is filled with unusual, many-colored formations of soil and rock.

Badlands National Park contains numerous plant and animal remains (fossils), such as footprints, leaves, and bones, from more than 25 million years ago. Many of these fossils reveal interesting things about the park's former animal life. For example, there was a pig that chewed its cud like a cow, a horse that was less than 2 feet tall, and a rhinoceros that was 12 feet tall. Sadly, modern animals like bears, elk, wolves, and bighorn sheep are also gone, the victims of too much hunting. Pronghorns, the fastest mammals in North America, live in the Badlands, along with prairie dogs, bison, meadowlarks, and golden eagles. Despite its dry climate, the Badlands has dozens of kinds of grasses and many wildflowers, but there are few trees.

Badlands National Park, with its strange and beautiful terrain, was given its name by the Sioux Indians because of the troubles they had in crossing the region.

South Dakota Highway 240 runs through the park for 25 miles. It has good views of the landscape, as does the Castle Trail. The Fossil Exhibit Trail, where casts of fossils are displayed, is a popular walk.

When large numbers of white people first came to the Badlands in the mid-1800s, the Sioux ruled the area. Sioux and whites fought, and in the end the Sioux were defeated. Portions of Badlands National Park are still owned by the Sioux. The White River Visitor Center features exhibits about them.

Isle Royale National Park

If you want to get away from it all, Isle Royale National Park in Michigan is the place to go. There are no cars or paved roads—the park can be reached only by boat or seaplane.

Isle Royale is located in northwestern Lake Superior, the world's largest freshwater lake. It consists of one large island, about two hundred smaller islands, and a lot of water. The main island is about 45 miles long and 9 miles across at its widest point. It has many ridges and valleys and a number of streams and lakes. Scientists say that the island is getting bigger at the rate of about 6 inches every hundred years. Counting land and water, the park makes up almost 572,000 acres.

With all its water, Isle Royale is a great place for fishing and boating. Hiking is also popular. The longest hiking trail is Greenstone Ridge Trail. Along the way, hikers pass 1,400-foot-high Mount Desor, the park's highest point. A much shorter trail goes to Lookout Louise, taking the hiker past curious rocks, beaches, and 4,000-year-old copper mines.

The tree-covered islands of Isle Royale are a wildlife lover's delight. There are beavers, mink, muskrat, foxes, snowshoe hares, moose, wolves, and more than two hundred different kinds of birds.

Despite its remote location, the Isle Royale area has long been of interest to people. Native Americans removed copper from the ancient mines by pounding the rock with stones. Much later, in the late 1600s, French explorers came through and gave the region its

name, which means "royal island." In the mid-1800s, American copper-mining companies were very active. Fur traders, lumbermen, and fishermen have also worked in Isle Royale. Fur traders killed so many beavers in the 1800s that the animal nearly became extinct there.

Congress passed the law creating Isle Royale National Park in 1931, but the park was not actually established until 1940.

Mammoth Cave National Park

Rivers and lakes are common sights in many areas of the country, but it is unusual to find them running underground. Not in Mammoth Cave! In Mammoth Cave, which lies within the more than 52,000 acres of Kentucky's Mammoth Cave National Park, there are two lakes, three rivers, and eight waterfalls that run underground in some places.

Mammoth Cave, with its many miles of corridors and five levels (one of which is 360 miles below the surface of the ground), is the largest cave system in the world. It got its name from the huge size (*mammoth* means "very big"). The cave began forming about 340 million years ago, when water started to dissolve the limestone rock. This slow process is still going on today.

Aboveground in and around Mammoth Cave National Park, you can see evidence of this process in the formation of *sinkholes*. These are holes in the ground that develop as water seeps through limestone. One such hole, Cedar Sink, is 150 feet deep and a

1/4 mile wide. Related to sinkholes are streams that come out of the ground, flow for a period of time, and then go underground again. Green River is one stream that does this. Underground, in Mammoth Cave, it is called Echo River.

Inside the cave, the combination of water, limestone, and air has produced many stonelike, colored formations. Those formed by water dripping from the ceiling are stalactites; those built up from the floor are stalagmites. Sometimes these formations take on unusual shapes. One formation, 75 feet high and 45 feet wide, resembles a frozen waterfall and is thus called Frozen Niagara. Others include the Macaroni Factory and the Great Wall of China.

Although there are more than 300 miles of underground passages in Mammoth Cave, only 12

Stalactites (shown here) and stalagmites are called dripstones because they are formed by groundwater that drips through caves.

People who visit Mammoth Cave National Park can explore Green River on a riverboat.

miles are open to visitors. Lights have been installed, and nearly all trips inside the cave are led by park rangers. Probably the most popular walk is the one to Frozen Niagara. Sixty feet below Frozen Niagara is Crystal Lake. On the Wind Cave Trail, a bit of crawling is required! The longest trip in the cave is the Echo River tour, part of which is made by boat.

There is wildlife both inside Mammoth Cave and above it. Fish swim in Echo River and elsewhere in the cave, bats and crickets live near the cave's entrances, and hundreds of birds live within the park.

The cave itself is home to a number of very strange creatures. Over many thousands of years, some of these animals have developed special features in response to the cave's darkness. Eyes are not important to the animals that live in Mammoth Cave, nor does color matter much. As a result, there are fish that are colorless and blind. In fact, creatures like crawfish have no eyes at all! Instead, they have light sensors in their tails. Blind spiders and beetles also live within the cave.

According to legend, a hunter discovered Mammoth Cave in 1798, when he chased a wounded bear into it. But, in fact, Native Americans had been mining the cave long before that. In 1935, the body of one miner was discovered in the cave. Scientists determined that he had been crushed by a boulder about 2,300 years before! Because of the conditions in the cave, his body was fairly well preserved. Today it is on display in the cave.

MAMMOTH CAVE JUNIOR PARK RANGERS

Every national park has a group of men and women known as park rangers. Among their many tasks are giving educational talks, leading walks, and taking care of the parks. Specially trained rangers also help fight fires.

Being a park ranger is an interesting job, especially if you like the outdoors. Of course, only adults can work as rangers. However, in some national parks, there is a special program for children ages six to thirteen who want to become junior rangers.

To become a junior ranger at Mammoth Cave National Park, you must complete four activities in the *Junior Ranger Activity Booklet for Mammoth Cave National Park*. (It costs $1 at the visitor center.) Some activities require you to answer questions about the park, figure out a coded message, draw a make-believe creature that could survive in Mammoth Cave, and complete the "Nature Trail Bingo" game in the booklet. You must also attend two ranger-led programs and walk a surface trail.

Once you have finished the activities, you hand in your booklet to a ranger. If you successfully complete the program, you receive a certificate and patch and become an official junior ranger.

During the War of 1812, the government used saltpeter (potassium nitrate) from Mammoth Cave to make gunpowder. In 1843, a local doctor thought the humid cave would be a good place to treat people with tuberculosis (a lung disease). He built eleven huts inside the cave for the patients. The doctor's idea was wrong, but two of the huts can still be seen today.

For many years, Mammoth Cave was privately owned. In 1930, the state of Kentucky purchased it and donated it to the U.S. government. In 1941, Mammoth Cave became a national park.

THE ROCKY MOUNTAIN STATES

Within the Rocky Mountain states of Idaho, Montana, Wyoming, Nevada, Utah, Colorado, Arizona, and New Mexico are fourteen national parks. Many of these parks, naturally, feature magnificent mountains. One of Colorado's parks is even called Rocky Mountain National Park, but lots of other attractions besides mountains await visitors. Grand Canyon National Park in Arizona is the site of the world's most spectacular canyon. Carlsbad Caverns in New Mexico has huge caves. Colorado's Mesa Verde contains Native American cliff dwellings, Utah parks have unusual rock formations, and Yellowstone is a place of many natural wonders.

Opposite:
The Grand Canyon is known for its enormous size and stunning beauty.

25

Glacier National Park

Often called the "crown of the continent," Glacier National Park is packed with dramatic mountain attractions, wildflowers, and lots of wildlife, lakes, and waterfalls. It extends over more than 1 million acres of northwestern Montana.

One billion years ago, this region was covered by a sea. Then, over millions of years, the earth went through great changes, and mountains were pushed up. Geologists—scientists who study the history of the earth—can identify rocks in the mountains that come from different periods in the earth's history.

But it was the glaciers that made the park what we see today. Glaciers are large, thick sheets of very slow-moving ice left over from the Ice Age that began

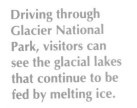

Driving through Glacier National Park, visitors can see the glacial lakes that continue to be fed by melting ice.

three million years ago. When the Ice Age ended and the climate became warmer, the glaciers in the park shrank. Today, their ice melts into streams faster than it can be replaced by snow and freezing rain. Two glaciers in the park that can be walked on are the Grinnell and Sperry glaciers. Each one covers about 300 acres.

The Going-to-the-Sun Road, a 50-mile road that twists and turns through the entire width of the park, offers breathtaking views of Rocky Mountain scenery. Especially striking are the lakes beneath the high peaks. Glacier National Park has more than two hundred lakes. Lake McDonald and Saint Mary Lake are the biggest.

The altitude of Glacier National Park varies from about 3,500 feet to more than 10,000 feet. Rainfall is heavier on the west side of the mountains than on the east. As a result, the park is rich in different kinds of trees and plants. In the west are forests of lodgepole pine, red cedar, hemlock, and other trees. On the drier eastern side are grass prairies and aspen trees.

Glacier is a paradise for wildflower lovers. Cream-colored blossoms of bear grass begin to appear in June. Bear grass is so common that it has become the park's official flower. Queencup, Indian paint-brush, and fireweed also abound.

Hundreds of birds and mammals and nearly two dozen kinds of fish can be found in Glacier National Park. Among the larger animals are moose, elk, deer, bighorn sheep, goats, and bears.

Glacier National Park is home to a wide variety of wildlife, including mountain goats.

Golden and bald eagles come to the park in the fall to feed on salmon. Trout is the most common fish. Fishing, along with camping, horseback riding, and boating, are all popular activities.

A Blackfoot Indian reservation adjoins the park's eastern boundary. The Blackfoot dominated the region from at least the 1700s to the late 1800s. By then, the buffalo herds they depended on for food and clothing had begun to disappear, and the Blackfoot began to starve. At the same time, prospectors thought the Glacier region might have gold, copper, and oil. They wanted to explore it. So in 1895, the Blackfoot sold what became the eastern part of the park to the U.S. government for $1.5 million.

The prospectors never found what they were looking for. Conservationists, however, appreciated the beauty of the area, and they teamed up with railroad owners who had recently extended a railroad line to what is now the town of West Glacier. The railroad wanted to attract tourists to the area. In 1910, conservationists and railroad owners persuaded Congress to create Glacier National Park.

Grand Canyon National Park

The National Park Service describes Grand Canyon National Park as "a land to humble the soul." The word *grand*, while telling something of the park's magnificence, cannot truly describe nature's wondrous creation. Rock walls, sometimes more than a mile high, are all colors of the rainbow, and their colors are continually changing. A 277-mile river flows between these walls, which are in some places separated from one another by just 1/2 mile and in other places by as much as 18 miles.

The Grand Canyon is located in northwestern Arizona. Flowing through the Grand Canyon on its way to the Gulf of California is the Colorado River. It is this river that, over the ages, helped to carve out such a magnificent canyon.

Riding down into the Grand Canyon on horseback is one of the most exciting ways to experience the canyon's beauty and its massive size.

The park is made up of the North Rim, the South Rim, and the canyon itself. On the North Rim are beautiful forests. Because of the winter snows, this section is closed for about six months a year. The South Rim is 1,000 feet lower in elevation, so it is warmer and drier. Even hotter is the very bottom of the canyon, down along the river, where summer temperatures often reach 110 degrees Fahrenheit.

Many people go to Grand Canyon National Park just to see the fabulous scenery, but visitors can also camp, ride horses and mules, and hike on hundreds of miles of trails. Hikers going down the canyon walls to the river have to remember that it is a long way back up! The popular Bright Angel Trail winds down 4,400 feet to the river from Grand Canyon Village on the South Rim. Hiking the entire trail takes at least 5 hours going down and 10 hours coming back.

Those who want more excitement can take raft or boat trips on the Colorado River. Going the whole way through the canyon requires several days. As it flows through the Grand Canyon, the river contains many thrilling—and sometimes dangerous—rapids.

The colored rock walls of the Grand Canyon are beautiful during daylight, and are even more spectacular at sunset.

Native Americans inhabited the region of the Grand Canyon as long as 4,000 years ago, and Indian tribes still live in the park. A Spaniard, Don García López de Cárdenas, was the first white person to discover the canyon, in 1540. In 1869, the American explorer John Wesley Powell became the first person to travel the Colorado River through the length of the canyon. This would be a remarkable achievement for anyone, but it was even more so for Powell, who had just one arm.

President Theodore Roosevelt was so impressed when he visited the Grand Canyon in 1903 that he told the American people: "Do nothing to mar its grandeur. Keep it for your children and your children's children, and all who come after you...." Roosevelt proclaimed the canyon a national monument in 1908. Then, in 1919, Congress established it as a national park. In 1975, its size was doubled to more than 1 million acres.

Yellowstone National Park

Stories of the wonders of Yellowstone began reaching the eastern United States in the mid-1800s. Many people regarded them as "tall tales." Who could believe reports of holes in the ground that suddenly shot forth boiling water, of bubbling colored mud, or of waterfalls higher than Niagara Falls? No doubt some stories told by returning explorers and animal trappers *were* exaggerated. But soon it became clear that many of them were true. The United States

The thermal activity of the hot springs and geysers in Yellowstone National Park was one of the reasons that people were first interested in preserving the area.

government sent a team of scientists to study the area. Their report, plus statements from Montana residents and other people, persuaded Congress in 1872 to make Yellowstone a national park.

Yellowstone, with its more than 2 million acres, is very large. Before 1980, when several enormous new parks were established in Alaska, and Alaska's Denali National Park was enlarged, Yellowstone was the largest.

Yellowstone is probably best known for its thousands of hot springs and geysers. In those places where there are geysers and hot springs, hot water and steam come out of the ground. This is known as thermal activity. Yellowstone National Park has more thermal-activity sites than any place on earth.

More than one hundred geysers regularly shoot forth water and steam in exciting bursts of energy. Yellowstone's Old Faithful, the most famous geyser in the world, erupts many times each day. Other geysers include Giant, Grotto, Castle, Riverside, and Lone Star. At the park's hot springs, hot water coming out of the ground mixes with clay. Sometimes, the clay has minerals in it that color the mixture. The result is a "paint pot" that can be strikingly beautiful. Algae, tiny plants that live in water, also add color to some of the hot springs. Notable among the hot springs are Mammoth Hot Springs and the Fountain Paint Pot.

Yellowstone Lake, the largest lake in North America at its altitude, is located within the park. It is nearly 8,000 feet above sea level and has a shoreline of more than 100 miles. People often fish and boat on the lake, but it is much too cold for swimming. The Yellowstone River flows through the lake.

North of the lake, the river flows over two waterfalls and into a magnificent canyon. The Upper Falls are more than 100 feet high, and the Lower Falls are more than 300 feet high. The canyon is called the Grand Canyon of the Yellowstone. It is 24 miles long and 1,500 feet deep in some places. The canyon's yellow, white, and orange walls are made of rock that came from a volcanic eruption millions of years ago. Trails

OLD FAITHFUL

Old Faithful is a very popular tourist attraction in Yellowstone National Park. It is probably the most famous geyser in the world, but it is not the park's biggest, most beautiful, or most powerful. Its popularity has resulted from the fact that it erupts at fairly regular intervals each day. That's how it got its name, Old Faithful.

What is a geyser? The term comes from the Icelandic word *geysa*, which means "to gush." And that is what geysers do: they gush forth steam and hot water. Geysers are different from hot

springs. Hot springs continuously send forth steam and water, but geysers gush, or "erupt," only every now and then. They are located where unusual conditions allow water to seep through underground cracks and come into contact with very hot rocks. The water eventually heats and turns to steam. The steam, in turn, blasts out the cooler water above it. When that happens, the geyser erupts.

It is usually difficult to know when a geyser will erupt. But Old Faithful is no ordinary geyser. For many years, Old Faithful erupted on an average of every 67 minutes. Earthquakes, however, have increased that time to 78 minutes. The time between eruptions has ranged between about a half hour to more than 2 hours.

Each eruption of Old Faithful lasts 2 to 5 minutes. The geyser may shoot out as much as 10,000 gallons of water in one eruption. The water may go as high as 170 feet in the air. Geologists believe that Old Faithful is between two and three hundred years old.

go along the top of both sides of the canyon and down the canyon to the river. Altogether, the park has about 1,000 miles of hiking trails.

Yellowstone is a great wildlife park, with its deer, elk, bison, trumpeter swans, and many other interesting animals. Hayden Valley is a good place to see the wildlife. Near the north entrance to the park, at Gardiner, Montana, is a desert, but most of the park is covered with forest. The best wildflower displays are near the canyon at altitudes of about 8,000 feet. The highest point in Yellowstone is Eagle Peak, at 11,358 feet.

The 142-mile Grand Loop Road links many of the attractions in the park. It goes right through Hayden Valley and follows the northwest shore of Yellowstone Lake, passing through several of the best areas of thermal activity.

Native Americans traveled across the region for thousands of years before white people arrived. They used black obsidian (a rock found in the area), and other materials to make valuable objects such as weapons. Some of these objects were eventually traded to places as far away as Ohio.

A huge fire swept through Yellowstone in 1988. Three quarters of a million acres were burned to some degree. Scientists and conservationists debated whether such fires should be fought or allowed to burn themselves out. Many experts now believe that fire is one of nature's ways to keep complicated plant and wildlife systems in balance.

CHAPTER

★ 4

THE PACIFIC STATES

Forty percent of the national parks in the United States lie within the five Pacific states—those states that have coasts on the Pacific Ocean. The parks in this area were established over a ninety-year period. The oldest are Sequoia and Yosemite in California, established in 1890. The newest, Channel Islands National Park in California, and all the Alaska parks except Denali, were established in 1980.

The variety of attractions in the Pacific parks is enormous. Four California parks boast the world's tallest and largest trees. Mount McKinley, in Alaska's Denali, is the highest mountain in North America. Crater Lake in Oregon's Crater Lake National Park is the deepest lake in the United States. Hawaii's two

Opposite:
The Seven Pools of Haleakala National Park in Hawaii, on the island of Maui.

parks, Haleakala and Hawaii Volcanoes, feature volcanoes. So does Lassen Volcanic National Park in California. Mount Rainier in Washington's Mount Rainier National Park is a huge mountain that was once a volcano. It last erupted 2,500 years ago.

Other beautiful sights in the Pacific parks include dramatic coastlines, rain forests, tall waterfalls, meadows of wildflowers, and glaciers. Among the many creatures in these parks are bears, moose, elk, sea lions, whales, and hundreds of birds.

Denali National Park

Denali means "the great one" in the Athapaskan language of the Native American people who were the first inhabitants of inland Alaska. What they called "Denali" we refer to as Mount McKinley. When the park was established in 1917, it was named Mount McKinley National Park. In 1980, however, Congress renamed it *Denali*. At that time, the park was also enlarged to three times its former size. Denali National Park now consists of nearly 5 million acres.

Mount McKinley is a famous attraction in Denali National Park. Its peak is 20,320 feet above sea level. A few miles southwest of it is another very high mountain, Mount Foraker, which is 17,400 feet high. About a dozen other mountains in the park, all part of the Alaska Range, are more than 10,000 feet high.

Because it is so far north—just 240 miles south of the Arctic Circle—Denali National Park is very cold. In winter, temperatures at the park headquarters

Because Mount McKinley is the highest mountain in all of North America, it is often referred to as the "top of the continent." Majestically rising above the ground in Alaska's Denali National Park, Mount McKinley is one of a group of mountains in the Alaska Range. It actually has two peaks, the North Peak and the South Peak, which are 2 miles apart. The North Peak is 19,470 feet above sea level, and the South Peak, the true summit, is 20,320 feet above sea level.

The South Peak was first climbed in 1913 by the Hudson Stuck expedition, which took fifty-three days to get to the top. Since then, many others have climbed the mountain. But more than one hundred have been injured, and many climbers have died.

Mount McKinley's weather is severe. The upper two thirds of the mountain, where the heads of many glaciers begin, is permanently covered by snow, and the winds gust to 100 miles an hour. Unfortunately for tourists, Mount McKinley is often under clouds.

The best times for viewing it are early morning and late afternoon. The Park Road in Denali National Park offers good viewing spots at Reflection Pond and Wonder Lake, where the mountain is reflected in the water.

The mountain was named for William McKinley, U.S. president from 1897 to 1901.

near Riley Creek go as low as -50 degrees Fahrenheit. Up in the mountains it is even colder. And, because the park is so far north, there are only 5 to 6 hours of daylight in December and January. During the short summer there may be up to 20 hours of daylight. Temperatures do not get very warm, however. The high is about 50 degrees Fahrenheit.

Denali National Park is a fabulous place to see wildlife. Observers have identified more than 150 kinds of birds and nearly 40 mammals. Some of the birds live in the park. One is the ptarmigan. This bird is brown and gray in spring and summer and white in winter. In winter, its feathers work as snowshoes to keep it from sinking into the snow. Among the larger animals in Denali are Dall sheep, Alaska moose, and grizzly bears.

Olympic National Park

Olympic National Park is in western Washington, not far from Seattle, the state's capital. A narrow section of the park's more than 900,000 acres borders on the Pacific Ocean, where waves crash against steep, rocky cliffs and huge boulders. But most of the park, with its magnificent rain forest, high mountains, and many glaciers, lies inland.

Olympic's wildlife includes salmon, bald eagles, spotted owls, mountain lions, and elk. In the autumn at Salmon Cascades you can see salmon jumping from one pool to another in the Soleduck River as they travel upstream to reproduce. Offshore, in fall and spring, you can see gray whales.

Portions of the park receive the heaviest rainfall in the United States outside Hawaii. There are Sitka spruce and red cedar trees up to 300 feet tall and 25 feet across. These trees are nearly as big as redwoods, the world's largest trees. Higher up in the park are other kinds of trees and meadows with beautiful wildflowers.

Higher still are the mountain peaks and about sixty glaciers. Mount Olympus, the highest mountain, is almost 8,000 feet high. In some years, more than 200 feet of snow fall on it! A good place for viewing the mountain is Hurricane Ridge, an excellent winter ski area.

Within the park's coastal section are three Native American villages, and a fourth village is nearby. The Indians are famous for their finely carved dugout canoes.

Olympic was made a national monument in 1909 and was established as a national park in 1938.

Rialto Beach, on the shoreline of Oympic National Park, offers dramatic views of offshore islands.

41

Yosemite National Park

Yosemite National Park embraces an immense tract of scenic wildlands in the Sierra Nevada Mountains in east central California. It features all kinds of natural wonders. Waterfalls, huge trees, wildflowers, high cliffs, and a wide variety of animals (mule deer, monarch butterflies, and black bears among them), can be found throughout Yosemite's nearly 800,000 acres.

The park offers three major features: an alpine (high) wilderness, Yosemite Valley, and groves of giant sequoia trees. Many of the sights in these areas and throughout the park can be seen from a car. There are 200 miles of roads in Yosemite. The eastern entrance to the park is at Tioga Pass. At 9,945 feet, Tioga Pass is the highest road in California. Yosemite also has about 800 miles of trails to walk on.

The high wilderness area ranges from 7,000 to more than 13,000 feet above sea level. Tuolumne Meadows, about 8,500 feet high, is famous for its wildflowers, which are at their peak in early summer.

Yosemite Valley, in the south central part of the park, is a canyon that was carved by glaciers millions of years ago. The Merced River runs through it, and cliffs like El Capitan and formations like Half Dome and

Half Dome, at the eastern end of Yosemite Valley, stands 8,852 feet high.

REDWOODS: THE WORLD'S BIGGEST TREES

The biggest trees in the world are redwoods. Thousands of years ago, they grew in many places, but today they are found in the western United States and central China.

Fortunately, these rare and wonderful trees grow in four of America's national parks—Kings Canyon, Redwood, Sequoia, and Yosemite—and in other protected areas of the United States. There, they cannot be cut down.

There are two kinds of redwoods in the United States: the coast redwood and the giant sequoia. The coast redwood is the larger of the two. Coast redwoods can be seen in Redwood National Park. Giant sequoias can be seen in Kings Canyon, Sequoia, and Yosemite national parks.

Coast redwoods are frequently 200 to 275 feet tall. One coast redwood, which stands on the bank of Redwood Creek in Redwood National Park, is 368 feet tall! The

trunks of coast redwoods are often 10 to 15 feet wide.

While giant sequoias may not be as tall as coast redwoods, they grow larger in diameter and bulk and weigh more. They are so enormous that road tunnels have been cut through some of them.

Sentinel Dome rise abruptly thousands of feet above the valley floor. Glacier Point, which is 3,200 feet above the valley, provides a magnificent view of the entire area. Of the many waterfalls in Yosemite Valley, Yosemite Falls, the highest in North America, is

probably the most famous. It has two parts: the Upper Falls and the Lower Falls. Together, water going over them drops almost 2,500 feet. The Upper Falls drops more than 1,400 feet—more than nine times the height of Niagara Falls. But the tallest single waterfall is Ribbon Falls, which drops 1,612 feet—a distance greater than the height of New York City's Empire State Building!

Yosemite has three groves of giant sequoia trees: Mariposa, Tuolumne, and Merced groves are near the park's western entrance. Sequoia trees are the largest living things in the world and are also very old. The Grizzly Giant in the Mariposa Grove is thought to be more than 2,500 years old.

Yosemite has an interesting history. The area was discovered in 1851, when Major James D. Savage and his men followed a band of raiding Yosemite Indians into their valley. Later, in the 1860s, California geologists began exploring the region and reported on its attractions. At that time, the U.S. government owned the land. In 1864, President Lincoln signed a law granting to California the Yosemite Valley and the Mariposa Grove "for all time." In effect, the law made Yosemite a California state park. It wasn't until 1890 that it became Yosemite National Park.

AMERICA'S NATIONAL PARKS

PARK	LOCATION	DATE ESTABLISHED	SIZE (ACRES)	SPECIAL FEATURES
Acadia	Maine	1929	41,888	Atlantic coast, high mountains, forests
Arches	Utah	1971	73,379	Giant arches
Badlands	South Dakota	1978	242,756	Strange land features, fossils
Big Bend	Texas	1944	801,163	Mountains, canyons, desert
Biscayne	Florida	1980	173,467	Semitropical islands, coral reefs
Canyonlands	Utah	1964	337,570	Colored rock formations, canyons, ancient cliff homes
Capitol Reef	Utah	1971	241,904	Colored rock formations, fossils
Carlsbad Caverns	New Mexico	1930	46,775	Deepest caves discovered to date
Channel Islands	California	1980	249,354	Marine and bird life
Crater Lake	Oregon	1902	183,224	Lake in extinct volcano crater
Dry Tortugas	Florida	1992	64,700	Large stone fort, marine and bird life
Everglades	Florida	1947	1,506,499	Semitropical wilderness
Gates of the Arctic	Alaska	1980	7,523,888	Above Arctic Circle, wilderness
General Grant	California	1890	461,901	Canyons, giant trees
Glacier	Montana	1910	1,013,572	Glaciers, many lakes
Glacier Bay	Alaska	1980	3,225,284	Glaciers, rain forest
Grand Canyon	Arizona	1919	1,218,375	Canyon of the Colorado River
Grand Teton	Wyoming	1929	309,993	High mountains
Great Basin	Nevada	1986	77,100	Very old bristlecone pines, Lehman Caves
Great Smoky Mountains	Tennessee, North Carolina	1934	520,269	Highest mountains in East, Appalachian culture
Guadalupe Mountains	Texas	1972	86,416	Desert, limestone fossil reef
Haleakala	Hawaii	1960	28,655	Extinct volcanic crater
Hawaii Volcanoes	Hawaii	1916	229,177	Active volcanoes
Hot Springs	Arkansas	1921	5,839	47 hot mineral springs
Isle Royale	Michigan	1940	571,790	Lake Superior, ancient copper mines

PARK	LOCATION	DATE ESTABLISHED	SIZE (ACRES)	SPECIAL FEATURES
Katmai	Alaska	1980	3,716,000	Mountains, rivers, marshlands
Kenai Fjords	Alaska	1980	669,541	Glaciers, fjords, major U.S. ice caps
Kobuk Valley	Alaska	1980	1,750,421	Arctic wildlife, Native American culture
Lake Clark	Alaska	1980	2,636,839	Lakes, volcanoes
Lassen Volcanic	California	1916	106,372	Volcanic activity
Mammoth Cave	Kentucky	1941	52,419	Cave system, underground rivers
Mesa Verde	Colorado	1906	52,122	Ancient cliff homes
Mt. McKinley (Denali)	Alaska	1917	4,716,726	Mt. McKinley, highest mountain in North America, glaciers
Mount Rainier	Washington	1899	235,613	Mountains, glaciers
National Park of American Samoa	American Samoa	1988	9,000	Tropical rain forests, coral reefs
North Cascades	Washington	1968	504,781	Mountains, glaciers
Olympic	Washington	1938	922,654	Rain forest, mountains, Pacific coast
Petrified Forest	Arizona	1962	93,533	Petrified trees, Painted Desert,
Redwood	California	1968	110,132	Giant trees, Pacific coast
Rocky Mountain	Colorado	1915	265,198	Rockies' Front Range
Sequoia	California	1890	402,482	Giant trees, Mount Whitney
Shenandoah	Virginia	1935	196,039	Skyline Drive, Blue Ridge Mountains
Theodore Roosevelt	North Dakota	1978	70,447	Roosevelt's ranch, unusual land shapes
Utah (Bryce Canyon)	Utah	1928	35,835	Colored rock formations
Virgin Islands	Virgin Islands	1956	14,689	Beaches, coral reefs
Voyageurs	Minnesota	1975	218,035	Forests, lakes
Wind Cave	South Dakota	1903	28,295	Caves, bison
Wrangell–St. Elias	Alaska	1980	8,331,604	Largest park, mountains, glaciers,
Yellowstone	Wyoming, Montana, Idaho	1872	2,219,791	First park, Old Faithful, hot springs, Grand canyon of the Yellowstone
Yosemite	California	1890	761,170	Granite domes, giant trees, high waterfalls
Zion	Utah	1919	146,598	Canyon and mesas

Where to Get More Information

To learn more about a particular national park, contact the main office of the National Park Service:

>National Park Service
>Main Interior Building, Room 2328
>P.O. Box 37127
>Washington, D.C. 20013-7127
>(202) 208-4648

The Park Service also operates ten regional offices. The main office can tell you which one is closest to you and how you can get in touch with it.

For Further Reading

Fisher, Christy, et al. *National Parks: A Kid's-Eye View: The Rocky Mountains.* Washington, D.C.: Starword Books, 1988.

Hallett, Bill, and Hallett, Jane. *National Park Service: Activities and Adventures for Kids.* Tucson, AZ: Look & See, 1991.

Mackintosh, Barry. *National Park Service.* New York: Chelsea House, 1988.

Scott, David L., and Scott, Kay W. *Guide to the National Park Areas: Eastern States.* Chester, CT: The Globe Pequot Press, 1987.

Scott, David L., and Scott, Kay W. *Guide to the National Park Areas: Western Areas.* Chester, CT: The Globe Pequot Press, 1987.

Index